Focus

Personal Mission

Self-discovery Workbook

LEADER | **Breakthru**

LEADERSHIP DEVELOPMENT
Workbooks

Each of our lives has purpose when seen in light of God and his purposes. God has created each of us to do good deeds which he authored into our lives, before time began (Ephesians 2:10).

The question is not whether God is at work IN OUR LIVES, but rather the discovery of his shaping work. This workbook series is designed to help you discover God forming our your life and how you can best join that work in the days ahead.

Perspective	Focus	Mentoring
PERSONAL TIME-LINE	**PERSONAL MISSION**	**PERSONAL MENTORS**

The **Perspective** *Workbook*

FOCUS is one of three steps that can help lead to greater clarity and focus in your life for Christ. Each step and workbook is designed to be self-discovery and bring new clarity and insight.

FOCUS will help you clarify and focus your life mission and development, and provide you a step-by-step process to developing a statement of your personal mission and calling.

The FOCUS PODCAST is an audio resource that helps to walk you through each step of the process of clarifying your mission and is the companion resource with this workbook. It can be obtained at the Leader Breakthru website:www.leaderbreakthru.com/lbu.focus.

All three steps of this leadership development series have been woven together into a powerful personal discovery process called... **Focused Living.**

Focused Living is available in a variety of forms:

Focused Living On-Line *(walk through an video, on-line process through each step of the process)*

Focused Living Small Group *(walk through the process with your group utilizing the on-line process and group notes)*

Focused Living Retreat *(walk through the process in a powerful large group setting or retreat setting with facilitator notes and resources.*

© 2013 Leader Breakthru / Terry Walling

Focus

Effective believers learn to continually bring focus to their lives and ministry.

Today, more than ever, believers like yourself are searching for ways to recognize the hand of God at work in their lives, and to know that their lives will count for the building of God's Kingdom. But the difficulty comes in knowing how to bring focus to one's life and knowing that the course direction one has chosen is truly designed by the Lord. A personal mission statement can help.

A personal calling statement is an individual's best understanding to date of God's unique process and work in his or her life. The key to developing an effective mission statement is to understand how God has been at work in one's life in the past, and then to develop a statement that becomes a dynamic guide for the future.

A Personal Calling Statement is the best understanding to date of God's unique processing and destiny for an individual. Good calling statements:
- reflect an individual's unique, personal destiny.
- blend together an individual's biblical purpose, life values and personal vision.
- assist an individual to better understand his/her role in the body of Christ.
- provide encouragement and perserverence in difficult times.
- provide decision making help for future life and ministry opportunities.

The Four Steps of Focus

Step 1—Anchoring
What has God taught you from His word?
Reviewing of your biblical calling and purpose as a believer.
Biblical purpose anchors your personal calling.

Step 2—Assessing
How has God shaped you in your past?
Understanding you past development and the life values as a believer.
(Note: If completed, work from **Perspective** workbook is used here)

Step 3—Discovering
What is God calling you to accomplish?
Discovering your personal vision provides direction for the future.

Step 4—Implementing
How do you plan to accomplish your personal calling?
Clarifying your roles and learning how to integrate related goals into your monthly schedule helps to ensure the achievement of your calling.

© CRM/Terry Walling

Finishing Well

The Bigger Picture

The heart cry of every genuine believer is to stand at the end and hear Christ say, "well done thou good and faithful servant." It is the reason behind seeking to live a focused life. A simple definition of finishing well: *To be more passionate and committed to Christ at the end of one's life than in the beginning.*

Focus continues your journey toward living a focused life that pleases God, and finishes well. Before you begin *Focus,* take a moment to evaluate your current behavior in light of five habits that help believers finish well.

There are FIVE HABITS that help enhance a believers capacity to finish well. They are one result of the research of Dr. J. Robert Clinton, Professor of Leadership at Fuller Seminary in Pasadena, California. Dr. Clinton has studied over 1200 biblical, historical and contemporary servants of God. Take the Five Habits Checklist below.

1. *Effective believers maintain a learning posture throughout their entire lives.*
   They never stop learning. Whether informally (reading, personal growth, projects, personal research), non-formally (workshops, seminars, conferences) or sometimes through formal training (continuing education, degree programs).

2. *Effective believers recognize mentoring as a priority.*
   They are committed to being mentored and mentoring others God brings their way.

3. **Effective believers have a dynamic statement of personal calling.**
   They allow God to continually shape their unique and ultimate contribution. A believer's calling typically emerges in late 30's and the ability to articulate it the 40's and 50's.
   This habit is the focus of this workbook and exercise.

4. *Effective believers experience repeated times of renewal.*
   Effective, godly servants develop intimacy with God which, in turn, overflows into all of their life and ministry.

5. Effective believers increasingly perceive their life in terms of a big-picture, lifetime perspective. They manifest a growing awareness of their sense of destiny.

The FIVE HABITS Checklist

INSTRUCTIONS: Read each statement on pp. 5-7, and check the number on the continuum that most accurately describes you. Check "0" if the statement on the left represents you; check "5" if you feel you are described better by the statement on the right. Numbers "1" through "4" reflect various positions between the two extremes.

1. I am often frustrated by the demands of the ministry and my lack of personal growth. |—|—✓—|—|—| 0 1 2 3 4 5   I am able to handle the daily pressures of the ministry and still find times for reflection and growth.

© CRM/Terry Walling

Five Habits Checklist—Section One

1. I have a desire to do some personal growth projects, but I seldom have the time or discipline necessary to do so.
   |—|—|—|—|—|
   0 1 2 3 4 5
   I view my personal development as a lifelong learning process and am regularly involved in study projects.

2. I hear of various workshops and seminars that others find helpful, but I seldom attend.
   |—|—|—|—|—|
   0 1 2 3 4 5
   I regularly attend workshops and seminars that help enhance my personal growth and development as a leader.

3. I am simply too busy or have little desire for continuing formal education.
   |—|—|—|—|—|
   0 1 2 3 4 5
   I enjoy my continuing education classes and am currently enrolled in an education program.

4. I do some things for myself, but I don't feel fulfilled or that I am growing as a person or leader.
   |—|—|—|—|—|
   0 1 2 3 4 5
   I work to develop the "whole" person and set improvement goals for wide areas of personal growth development.

Section One Total ☐

Five Habits Checklist—Section Two

1. I feel overwhelmed by the needs of the ministry and seldom, if ever, spend time developing new leaders.
   |—|—|—|—|—|
   0 1 2 3 4 5
   I am always in the process of developing a pool of new leaders to release into ministry.

2. It is often hard for me to imagine that I have something to offer in a mentoring relationship to others.
   |—|—|—|—|—|
   0 1 2 3 4 5
   I generally have a good estimation of the strengths and abilities I can offer to other leaders.

3. I feel "alone" in the ministry and feel there are few who are helping me grow.
   |—|—|—|—|—|
   0 1 2 3 4 5
   I deeply value others and have a regular series of relationships that help me grow and develop.

4. I don't know what my actual developmental needs are or how a mentor could help.
   |—|—|—|—|—|
   0 1 2 3 4 5
   I view my development as a high priority and have obtained mentors to help ensure my ongoing growth.

Section Two Total ☐

© CRM/Terry Walling

Five Habits Checklist—Section Three

1. I often feel frustrated, wondering if I am doing what God really intends for me.
   |—|—|—|—|—|
   0   1   2   3   4   5
   I feel the things I do every day are meaningful and part of my biblical purpose and reason for existence.

2. I sometimes get glimpses of what I should do with my life, but somehow these visionary moments get lost in busy activity.
   |—|—|—|—|—|
   0   1   2   3   4   5
   I have thought deeply about why I exist as a person and have clarified my personal vision and what God is calling me to accomplish.

3. I often work based upon the need of the moment as opposed to a clear philosophy of ministry.
   |—|—|—|—|—|
   0   1   2   3   4   5
   I am able to decide what is important for me to do, basing my decisions upon a clear ministry philosophy.

4. I am easily frustrated by changes in the direction of ministry or in my life situation.
   |—|—|—|—|—|
   0   1   2   3   4   5
   I feel like I have a clear direction, but I allow God to teach me new things and alter how I should minister.

Section Three Total ☐

Five Habits Checklist—Section Four

1. I nearly always feel "buried," having more to do than I can handle. Getting away for me seems impossible.
   |—|—|—|—|—|
   0   1   2   3   4   5
   I regularly schedule times away for personal retreat and reflection.

2. I feel that "personal" time is selfish, especially when I am called to help minister to others.
   |—|—|—|—|—|
   0   1   2   3   4   5
   I feel an investment in my personal walk with Christ will cause me to experience deeper intimacy with Christ and greater effectiveness.

3. If someone were to ask me how long has it been since I have felt the presence of God, I'd have to respond, "Quite some time."
   |—|—|—|—|—|
   0   1   2   3   4   5
   I regularly experience times of renewal and freshness in my walk and intimacy with Christ.

4. Although I know the spiritual disciplines are important to real growth, I seldom have time to focus on them.
   |—|—|—|—|—|
   0   1   2   3   4   5
   My walk with Christ is greatly enhanced through regular usage of a variety of spiritual disciplines.

Section Four Total ☐

© CRM/Terry Walling

Five Habits Checklist—Section Five

1. I have trouble rising above the current circumstances to get a big-picture perspective on my life.

   |—|—|—|—|—|
   0   1   2   3   4   5

   I earnestly try to understand my current circumstance in light of what God has been doing over my lifetime.

2. I realize that God is shaping my life, but I seldom am able to understand how He is at work in my life.

   |—|—|—|—|—|
   0   1   2   3   4   5

   I feel that the things that happen to me every day are part of God's development of my life, and I can recognize patterns of His work.

3. I have trouble trying to keep track of the many areas of my life: home, office, etc.

   |—|—|—|—|—|
   0   1   2   3   4   5

   I feel a sense of order in my life because I am able to regularly gain perspective on my life.

4. I hear other leaders talk about their calling and vision, but I rarely feel I have a sense of destiny.

   |—|—|—|—|—|
   0   1   2   3   4   5

   In my times with Christ, I continue to sense a unique, personal destiny that He has for my life.

   Section Five Total ☐

Summary

Go back and total your score in each section. Record your totals in the boxes. Review your scores. Where are you strong? Weak? Look at your scores in relationship to each other.

- Habit #1 (lifelong learning) and Habit #4 (repeated times of renewal) are attitudes that a believer must commit to maintain if they are to finish well.
- Habit #5 (perspective), **Habit #3 (personal calling)** and Habit #2 (mentoring) are the three steps that comprise the *Focused Living* process.

1. Maintains a learning posture throughout life.   Section One Total ☐
2. Commitment to being mentored and mentoring.   Section Two Total ☐
3. **Dynamic personal mission and calling.**   **Section Three Total** ☐
4. Repeated times of personal renewal.   Section Four Total ☐
5. Lifetime, big-picture perspective   Section Five Total ☐

This workbook, **Focus** provides help with the third habit.
The **Focused Living** process is designed to help you intentionalize the five habits into your life.

© CRM/Terry Walling

STEP 1 Focus
Anchoring Your Call

Defining Terms

Before we beign the process of creating a statement of your personal calling, review the following definitions that will be used throughout this workbook.

- **Biblical purpose** describes our biblical reason for existence.
- **Values** describes our inherent preferences, assumptions, and beliefs.
- **Vision** is a word-picture of a preferable future from God's perspective.
- **Roles** refer to the unique tasks we are called and best equipped to fulfil.
- **Goals** are faith statements that help provide accountability for vision.
- **Personal Calling statement** is a summation statement that integrates biblical purpose, life-ministry values, and personal vision.

Step One of the pesonal calling process challenges you back into God's Word, and a search of the scriptures which reveal God's ultimate purpose for all of our lives.

You will need ... Bible; possible concordance
Time required ... Approximately 1-2 hours.

ANCHORING ASSESSING DISCOVERING IMPLEMENTING WHERE DO WE GO FROM HERE?

© CRM/Terry Walling

STEP 1

Foundation of Personal Calling

Destiny

Esther ... if I perish, I perish." (Esther 4:16)
John Knox cried for a nation, "Give me Scotland or I shall die."
Martin Luther saw a reformation of the church and a gospel of grace through faith.

At the core of a personal calling is the concept of **destiny.**

Personal calling (or mission) presupposes a unique, personal destiny for each of us.

God has brought each of us into existence, at this point in time, to bring glory to His name and to fulfil ourpart in the expansion of His Kingdom.

Destiny is the living out of God's purposes in one's own generation. Paul said of David, "For when David had served God's purposes in his own generation, he fell asleep" (Acts 13:36).

The Lord told Jeremiah, "Before I formed you in the womb I knew you. Before you were born I set you apart; I appointed you as a prophet to the nations" (Jeremiah 1:5). Jeremiah had a unique destiny to fulfill.

Jesus obviously lived with a sense of purpose and destiny. Jesus said, "My food is to do the will of Him who sent me and to finish His work" (John 4:34). On the cross He cried out, "It is finished" (John 19:30). Jesus' life had purpose. Jesus came to die. His death on the cross completed what He had come to do. His resolve was to live out His own personal destiny. This focus caused Him to make daily choices in line with His personal mission.

Paul, too, lived with a sense of destiny and purpose. In Romans 15:16, Paul reflects on his call "to be a minister of Christ Jesus to the Gentiles ... so that the Gentiles might become an offering acceptable to God."

In Ephesians 2:10, Paul reminds each of us that we are God's craftsmanship, "created in Christ Jesus to do good works, which God prepared in advance for us to do."

Our Uniqueness

Each of us is called by God to live out our godly purposes, to love and worship Him, to share His love with one another and a hurting world, to glorify the God and Father of our Lord Jesus Christ (Romans 15:6).

But we also have been gifted to play a specific role as members of Christ's body. Throughout history, God has called his servants to use their gifts and abilities to influence the hearts and lives of their generation. Destiny processing is believers' ability to focus his or her ministry according to God's unique call on his or her lives.

© CRM/Terry Walling

Where it Begins!

Living a focused life requires a solid foundation.
Scripture reveals to each believer both why he or she exists, and gives guidance for the journey. A proper Biblical foundation provides the "true north" for every believer.

Clarifying Biblical purpose helps a believer in three ways:
- It declares why you exist. It captures the heart of why you are on this planet and what it means to live in relationship with God.
- It defines your life not by what you think, but by what God thinks. It anchors your life in the character of your creator.
- It clarifies the non-negotiable. It tells what never changes about who you are, regardless of the circumstances.

Joshua stated it for his life... "as for me and my house, we wills serve the Lord."
Joshua 24:15

Paul declared it for his life... "to know Christ, and the power of His resurrection."
Philippians 3:10

Verses that Guide Your Life

Take a moment and list the verses that God has used to guide your life. They are verses that remind you what is most important. Often, these are the verses that we turn to when we are confused, or when we feel like we are lost. List the verse, then summarize what is important from each verse.

Verse   **What it says to you ... What's Important?**

1. _____   _____

2. _____   _____

3. _____   _____

4. _____   _____

5. _____   _____

6. _____   _____

© CRM/Terry Walling

Biblical Purpose

Take your Bible and review the following verses. Each of the following verses highlights a biblical mandate given to every believer.

FIRST, Summarize each verse in your own words.
SECOND: Reflect on what the verse says about the given topic.

1. Matthew 28: 18-20

   EVANGELISM

2. Matthew 22: 37-40

   PASSION FOR GOD
   PASSION FOR OTHERS

3. Psalm 34:1-3

   WORSHIP

4. Colossians 2:6,7

   SPIRITUAL GROWTH

5. Isaiah 58:6-12

   SERVICE

Many more Scriptures could have been reviewed. These verses serve to summarize the Biblical mandates given to every believer. God calls each believer to a holy calling. It is a life focused not just on doing, but being. What we do flows out of who we are.

Based on your Scriptural reflection on p. 10 and p. 11, use these questions to help you think through God's purpose for your life.

- Why do I exist as a person? Why did God create me?
- What does God say provides man's greatest fulfillment?
- What is my response to God's work of grace and salvation on my behalf?

© CRM/Terry Walling

Writing Out Your Biblical Purpose

Exercise

Examples of a Biblical Purpose

My purpose is to bring glory to my Lord and Savior Jesus Christ through consistent worship of Him with my praise and my life, to cultivate a life of intimacy with Jesus that will reflect His love and grace of God to my world.

The purpose of my life is to know God and to hear His voice so clearly that I live a life of servanthood and obedience.

I live to glorify my Lord and Savior Jesus Christ (Romans 15:5,6).
I seek to personally experience the grace and truth of the Gospel (John 1:14), in order to demonstrate an authentic walk with Christ to believers ensnared in religion and unbelievers trapped in darkness.

Some Tips for writing out your Biblical purpose

- Be concise. It does not have to be long.
- Focus more on "being" as opposed to "doing." Doing will come out more in vision.
- Say it in a way that grips you, and declares why you exist as a person.

Write our your statement of Biblical Purpose in the box below.

Biblical Purpose

Transfer your biblical purpose statement to the summary sheet found on p. 17.

© CRM/Terry Walling

STEP 2 Focus
Assessing Your Past

Your Unique Development

David declared in Psalm 139 that each of us is "fearfully and wonderfully made." The next step in creating your personal mission statement is reflecting on your unique shaping as a believer.

The identification of life values helps express the unique ways in which God has shaped your life. Some experiences have been positive, some have been difficult, but all have contributed to the development of a unique set of convictions and principles which we call values.

(NOTE: If you have completed the creation of life values in *Perspective,* the *Focused Living* workbook, you may transfer your values on to p. 17.)

You will need ... Values and Time-line (if created)

Time required ... Approximately 1-2 hours

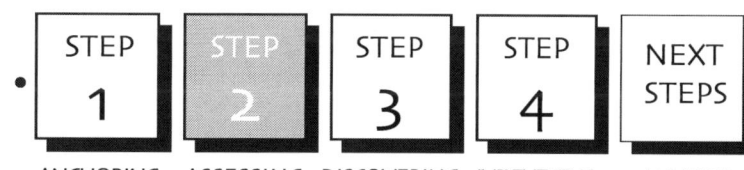

© CRM/Terry Walling

Focus
STEP 2
Reflecting On Your Past

Today, more than ever, believers are searching for ways to recognize the hand of God at work in their lives. To see again that the God of the universe is personally involved in our lives, brings hope and a greater desire to persevere through the turbulent days in which we live.

Most people feel their lives are pretty common.
It is not until believers gain a big-picture look at their lives that they begin to recognize God's unique, sovereign, shaping work.

God has been at work in ways that might previously have gone unnoticed. It is very easy to lose sight of the big-picture when we are entrenched in the day-to-day challenges of life.

A personal time-line is a big-picture overview of your life. It is a chronological map of a believer's development, highlighting those critical incidents and circumstances that God has used to shape character and purpose.

The **Life Graph** is a simple exercise that helps a believer gain greater perspective on his or her life. The **Life Graph** will help identify major chapters and insights to a believers development. See example below.

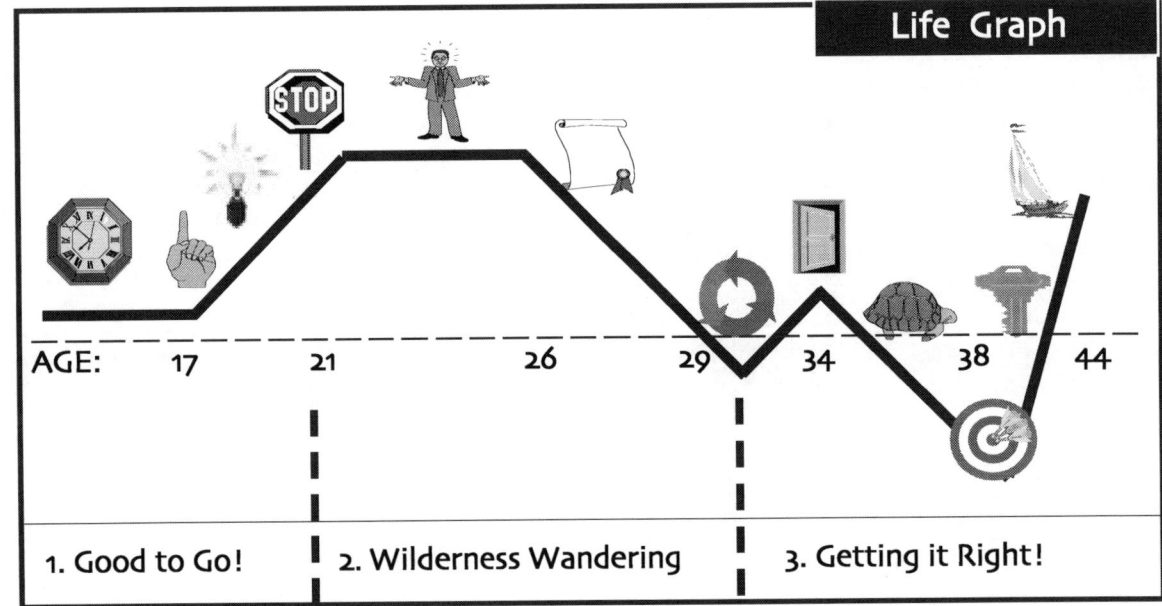

© CRM/Terry Walling

14

Creating Your Life Graph

Exercise

Three Steps

1. Draw a line graph that depicts the ups-and-downs of your life. The dotted line should be seen as the base-line for your life. Plot the ages on dotted line.
2. Create symbols to depict the major events that were occurring in your life during the various stages of your life graph.
3. Name each chapter in the box at bottom of graph. Choose names that describe what was occurring in your life, and what you believe God was doing.

Some Tips:
- Use your own symbols. Don't worry about not being an artist. Use symbols that work for you.
- God sometimes speaks the loudest during those moments that are the hardest. Reflect both the good and the difficult events on your life graph.

Life Graph

AGE:

Based on Life Graph, use the following questions to help you assess your past.

- What are some of the important lessons God has taught you about your character?
- What are some important lessons God has taught you about the balance of work and your personal life?
- What are some of your core convictions about people and relationships?
- What are some important lessons and insights God has taught you about your contribution?
- If you were to write the next chapter of your life, what would it include?

© CRM/Terry Walling

What's Important?

Based upon your review of your life and development up to this point, what is important? what are some of your core convictions about life and how you should live? In the space below, brainstorm about some of things that God has shown you to be important for your life. They do not need to be listed in a certain order.

1. _____
2. _____
3. _____
4. _____
5. _____
6. _____
7. _____
8. _____

Life Values

Values reflect an individual's unique beliefs, core convictions and guiding principles. Although believers can value many things, effective laborers learn to identify six to ten <u>core values</u> that reflect past processing experiences. One individual's values are stated below as an example:

People first:	My wife and family are my significant ministry. My capacity to influence requires the maintaining of relationships.
Being before doing:	It is easier to do, but it is more important to be. God cares about the process and the journey.
Team:	Doing life and work alone proves nothing.
Mentoring:	I value learning and a teachable spirit. I value the mentoring and resourcing of others.
The kingdom:	Jesus desires more and better disciples.
The Local church:	It is God's chosen vehicle for today. My involvement is critical.
Leadership:	Everything rises and falls on leadership.
Change:	A changeless gospel must confront a changing world.
Faith:	Life today requires both strength and courage.
Relevancy:	Meaningful ministry at work and in my neighborhood.

© CRM/Terry Walling

Writing Out Your Values

Exercise

Based upon your work in this step, write out your six to eight core values in the space below. Reminder: Values should be concise statements, reflecting your core convictions and principles. (Note: If you have completed your values in the *Perspective* workbook, transfer onto this page and continue to Step 3.)

Life Values

1.

2.

3.

4.

5.

6.

7.

8.

Transfer your life values to the summary sheet found on p. 24.

© CRM/Terry Walling

STEP 3 Focus
Discovering Your Future

Discovering the Future from God's Perspective

At the core of a personal calling is vision.

Vision is the ability to see the future from God's perspective.
Vision is God's preferable future. It flows from the redemptive heart of the Father.

Personal vision focuses on the next chapter of development for a believer; it gives words to the future.

Some struggle with the concept of vision.
Many have abused vision in order to live out selfish ambitions.

But throughout history, God has birthed His plans into the hearts and lives of committed followers. From Moses to Hannah to Nehemiah to the Apostle Paul to Luther down to today. Personal vision is well documented on the pages of biblical and contemporary history.

You will need ... Work completed in steps one and two

Time required ... Approximately 2-4 hours.

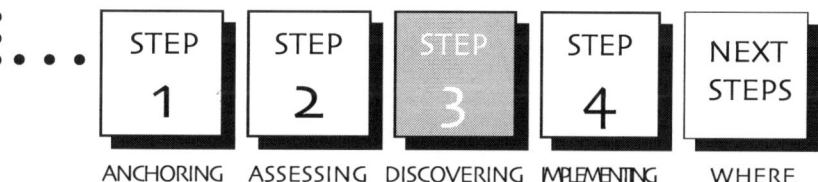

© CRM/Terry Walling

STEP 3

Personal Vision
God's Preferable Future

Vision is the ability to see God's preferable future.
It captures in a word picture what God wants to accomplish through the unique shaping of our lives.

Vision is heartbeat of the personal calling statement.
God designs it, we discover it.

Vision ignites passion! It motivates and captures a believer. It describes what the heart yearns to see accomplished and what would drive a believer to sacrificial living and obedience. Personal vision dares to answer questions like: *If you knew that you would not fail, what would you do in your lifetime for the glory of God?*

Vision comes into focus over time.
Like a Polaroid snapshot picture, vision is dynamic and revealed over time.
It is like a portrait that is painted on the canvas of our lives over a life time.
It is like Nehemiah, walking amongst the ruins of Jerusalem, not just planning the rebuilding project, but picturing in his mind a rebuilt wall with men and women once again worshipping God. As he worked, the vision became more vivid and real.

Vision is different than purpose or mission.
Purpose clarifies, but vision gives motivation.
Purpose gives meaning, while vision describes contribution.
Purpose is more generic, applying to many.
Vision is specific and unique.

A Note About Ambition:
Many of us have pursued ambition, but called it vision. It was our own great dream for God.

Ambition is all about me.
Calling is about alignment and obedience to God and His plan.
Discovering vision is not dreaming up your biggest dream, it is discovering what God has created and called you to do. Personal vision is about discovering what God has created me to do and surrendering to it.

© CRM/Terry Walling

Personal Vision

Exercise

Answering these questions will help you discover your personal vision.

1. The people and circumstances that have most shaped my life are …
   Parents, Mike McQuitty, FFC, college ministry, Kate,

2. When I think about ministry in the future, the area of ministry I would love to concentrate upon is __Discipling ministry leaders__. Why? I knew so little, I have learned so much and I love teaching others

3. The qualities of character I most admire and desire for God to shape into my life are…
   __humility, dependence, & compassion__ Why?
   I have seen pride destroy relationships, independence lead to burn out + self-satisfaction override the kingdom mission.

4. People who know me well believe I am most used by God when I am involved in __connecting others with missions & coaching__. Why?
   I have seen the most fruit in those areas.

5. My activities that contribute most to God's kingdom are __coaching my interns & teaching__. Why?
   I have seen my interns grow in their desires and abilities to serve. Teaching is new but I have seen great feedback and new results.

6. From the perspective of my personal life, my activities that I feel are making the greatest contribution to God's kingdom are __bringing others in__. Why?
   Many people are looking for community, role models, and every day examples.

7. Though I may have dismissed the thought many times for various reasons, at times I have felt I really should be doing __College Ministry!__ Why?
   At first, I thought I was just going to work a secular job and serve at church but God changed it all!

8. When people talk about a passion for ministry, I often begin to think about giving my life to accomplishing __a great ministry at SU__. Why? It is what I love and everything I think about.

> NOTE: Personal vision is an exercise in future perfect thinking. It is discerning influences that have created a passion for God and a passion to accomplish something

© CRM/Terry Walling

Personal Vision Draft
your best understanding to date

Vision requires time for reflection and processing, as well as the faith to embrace it. Therefore, set aside time for discerning your vision. Using your answers to the questions on p. 20, spend time in prayer and reflection, and begin to journal your thoughts.

Based upon the way God has shaped you in your past, what do you believe he is calling you <u>to be</u> and <u>to do</u> for his glory?

Testing Your Vision:
- Can you see it?
- Is it bigger than you?
- Does it engage your passion?
- Is it anchored in your past?
- Would you do it even if you did not get paid for it or had to pay for the chance to do it?

© CRM/Terry Walling

Vision Examples

"My vision is that people whose lives and spirits are enslaved by poverty would experience the love of Jesus as I use my passion for garage sales as a way to meet their needs and provide hope."

...Name unknown

"*I know* that God desires to use me to give our children the resources they need emotionally, spiritually, experientially, and financially in order to move into adulthood and make their faith their own.

I know God has placed me as a teacher to be a light in a dark place and to give my students the chance for a better life.

I believe God wants to use me to resource church leaders so that they would not be working from a deficit position but from one of hope and courage."

...Margaret

"I will endeavor to build a support structure for women in our church that will encourage them in their roles as wives, mothers, sisters, and daughters.

And I will participate in a training program for small group leaders, identifying, encouraging, and growing other leaders within the church. As a result, this ministry will impact the life of every church member, bringing each to a greater understanding of Christ's love and uniting the body to a greater effectiveness for the glory of God."

...Sarah

"As a result of my calling and my own unique giftedness, I have committed my life to raising a family that loves God and models a genuine believable faith. I desire to intentionally help my wife discover her place in ministry and grow in her effectiveness; spending time building up, encouraging and empowering our children.

I also dedicate myself to extending the kingdom of God through refocusing mission-based, Christ-centered local churches and developing relational support systems that will mentor and empower a new generation of leaders. I desire to impact 1000 churches and 1000 leaders into the 21st century."

...Terry

"For the remainder of my life, I am committed to building teams which strive to accomplish amazing things for the kingdom of God. Whether it be financial resources, civic influence, experiential wisdom, or accountability, I will contribute my part to the team: strength, stability, and a sense of encouragement that can only come from God's hand."

...Jeff

© CRM/Terry Walling

Personal Calling Statement

A statement of personal calling is a leader's best understanding to date of his oe her unique, personal destiny.

It is a holistic statement that integrates what a leader understands God has called him to be and to do for his glory.

A Personal Calling Statement is a dynamic statement reflecting your best understanding to date of what God is calling you to be and do in your future.

Over time, as a believer refines his or her statement of calling, it becomes a very unique document, reflecting the style, perspective, and growing insight of that leader. However, at the core it is a simple document that integrates the work you have now completed.

Effective calling statements have three clear, yet integrated components; biblical purpose, life values and personal vision. Sample calling statements are found on p. 25.

Personal calling statements bring three roads together into one, future direction.
It describes why you exist, who God has shaped you to be, and what God is calling you to accomplish. It is a compass to lead you into the future.

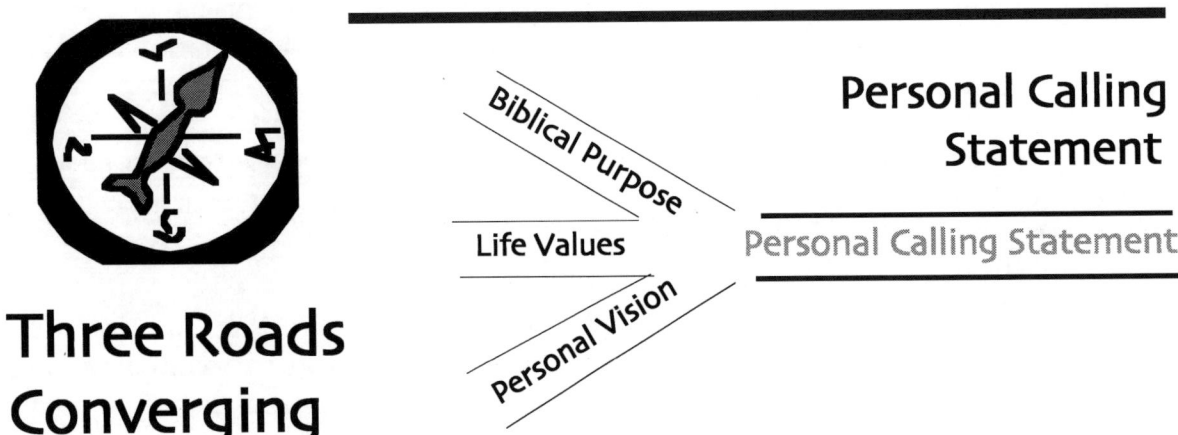

Three Roads Converging

Ultimately, your personal calling is lived out through:
- the roles you choose
- intentionalizing your development through goals and placing in your calendar
- identifying and pursuing mentors who will assist your growth and development

© CRM/Terry Walling

Personal Calling Statement:

First Draft

1st: Copy your Biblical Purpose in this box at the top of the page. *(p. 12)*

> I live to serve God through teaching + discipleship (Colossians 1:28-29 & Psalm 145:4)
>
> I see needs in the lives of people around and I am moved by compassion to serve them (Matt. 9:36)

2nd: Copy your values into the center portion of the page. *(p. 17)*

1. **College Students** — A critical + strategic time to evangelize + disciple
2. **Family** — I want the best for my wife & family
3. **Humility** — I cannot grow & learn without it.
4. **Missions** — We are called to obey + go!
5. **Discipleship** — We need to be challenged to grow.
6. **Authenticity** — I want to be the real deal
7. **Growth** — I need more every day
8.

3rd: Write your vision statement into this bottom box. *(p. 21)*

NOTE: This is an ideal time to incorporate refinements as a result of the feedback and further thinking.

> God has called me to serve in college ministry in order to bring others into community with Him. I am placed at Syracuse University in order to coach & train new Christian leaders for service in a variety of mission fields and to serve with humility, dependence on God, & full of compassion

date: 11/17/16

© CRM/Terry Walling

Personal Calling Statement
EXAMPLE

PURPOSE

I live to glorify my Lord and Savior Jesus Christ (Romans 15:5,6).
I seek to personally experience the grace and truth of the Gospel (John 1:14), in order to demonstrate an authentic walk with Christ to believers ensnared in religion and unbelievers trapped in darkness.

I daily seek to live in the present, and to practice the presence of Christ.
To love life as it unfolds as well as to live out my ultimate destiny.
I will not miss out and I cannot fail if I daily surrender my life to Christ.

VALUES

- <u>People</u> - My capacity to influence is based on relationship more than expertise
- <u>Being and doing</u> - It is easier to do, but it is more important to be
- <u>Learning Communities</u> - Doing life and ministry together
- <u>Family</u> - My wife and kids are my significant ministry
- <u>Continuous Improvement</u> - I value modeling a teachable spirit and doing it better
- <u>Kingdom Advance</u> - Jesus desires more and better disciples
- <u>Healthy local churches</u> - God's chosen vehicle today of light for a darkened world
- <u>Authentic Leadership</u> - Everything rises and falls on real leaders
- <u>Life-Change</u> - Taking the next step in a walk with Jesus Christ
- <u>Bravehearts</u> - Hope... Courage ... Seizing the day... taking the land

VISION

As I journey with Christ, I dedicate myself to creating:
- A safe-place within myself (personal care and growth).
- A safe-place within our home (intentional time with my wife and kids)
- A safe-place with a group of friends or colleagues (transparency and accountability)
- A series of safe-places for godly leaders, through the development of resources and supportive learning environments.

I dedicate myself to extending the kingdom of God through the refocusing of leaders and local churches, helping them to realize and live out all of what God intended.

© CRM/Terry Walling

STEP 4 Focus
Implementing Your Calling

The Keys to Implementation

Personal calling statements are often created and shelved. Unless your statement works itself into your daily schedule, it may be set aside, a casualty of your busy life.

Personal calling statements become useable documents when they are intentionally integrated into your calendar system. The key to linking your statement to your calendar involves determining your life roles and then developing your yearly goals into your weekly schedule.

Steps to integration:

1. Defining yourself
2. Defining your roles
3. Determining your yearly objectives
4. Deciding to Integrate into your calendar

You will need ... Personal Calling Statement and your calendar

Time required ... Approximately 2 hours.

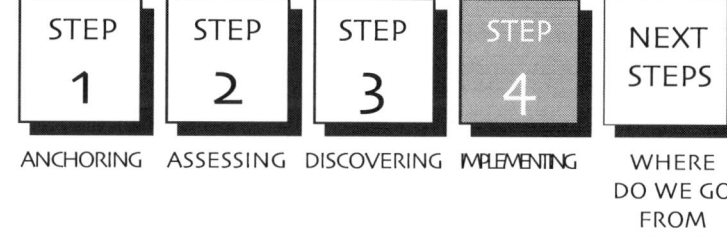

© CRM/Terry Walling

STEP 4
Implementing Your Personal Calling

DEFINITIONS

Acquired skills refer to those capacities, talents or aptitudes which have been learned by a person in order to allow him/her to accomplish a task or assignment.

Natural abilities refer to those capacities, skills, talents or aptitudes which are innate in a person and allow him/her to accomplish something.

A **spiritual gift** is a God-given unique capacity imparted to each believer for the purpose of releasing a Spirit empowered ministry via that believer.

Personality Types: Your uniqueness described by four predominant categories of personality:

1. **Task-oriented people** enjoy results. They are determined. He/she values productivity, is usually optimistic, and can be insensitive to the feelings of those he/she leads.

2. **Influence-oriented people** enjoy influencing others to achieve results. He/she is relational, idealistic, and very expressive in nature. He/she often seeks approval, is people-oriented, and can lack a disciplined lifestyle.

3. **Team-oriented people** enjoy participating with others. He/she is adaptive, realistic, and often very loyal. He/she is often more of a servant-specialist worker and can become too much of a spectator and dependent on others.

4. **Detail-oriented people** enjoy jobs that are done well and completed. He/she tends to be analytical and drawn to administrative issues. He/she is reflective and correct, but can become skeptical and judgmental.

Life roles refer to those roles that are a part of who we are as people and often deal with the significant relationships in our lives.

Steps to IMPLEMENTING your Personal Calling:

Step 1	Defining Yourself
Step 2	Defining Your Roles
Step 3	Determining Your Yearly Objectives
Step 4	Deciding to Integrate into Your Calendar

© CRM/Terry Walling

Influence Elements

Leadership is influence.

Believers bring about Godly influence through three means of influence. These are called "influence elements." Definitions of the three categories of influence elements are on p. 27. Examples of the three Influence Elements are provided below.

INFLUENCE ELEMENTS

ELEMENTS	EXAMPLES
SPIRITUAL GIFTS	(See Romans 12, 1 Corinthians 12 and Ephesians 4)
Word Gifts	teaching, exhortation, prophecy, apostleship pastor, evangelism, ruling
Power Gifts	word of wisdom, word of knowledge, faith, healings, discerning spirits, tongues, interpretation
Love Gifts	giving, mercy, helps, governments
NATURAL ABILITIES	
Creative	artistic, drama, design, musical, drawing
Cognitive	problem solving, analytical, intuitive, strategic thinking, system development
Relational	inspire, visual-written-verbal communication, team building, sensitive, visioning, persuasive, social, event planning
Physical Dexterity	athletics, physical, craftsman
ACQUIRED SKILLS	
Creative	artistic, drama, musical, painting, graphics, design
Cognitive	observation-analytical, training design, goal setting, Bible study skills, presenting
Relational Support	leadership, mentoring, public communication, linguistic, marketing, conflict resolution, group dynamics, consensus building, vision casting, motivating, coaching, selecting-developing leaders training, consulting, design of systems and structures, counseling
Analytical Skills	diagnostic, analyzing, synthesizing
Technical Skills	computer, accounting, programing

© CRM/Terry Walling

Who Are You?

Exercise

**TOP THREE
INFLUENCE ELEMENTS**

Using the definitions on p. 27 and the examples on p. 28, find a partner to help you better understand who you are, using the three influence elements.

Discuss the following with your partner:

- Reflect on major MINISTRY-JOB ASSIGNMENTS you have had as a believer. What reoccurring spiritual gifts, natural abilities and acquired skills do these assignments reveal.

    It may be helpful to list out your ministry assignments on a separate piece of paper and brainstorm what occurred during each ministry assignment in each of the three categories of influence elements.

- Together, select 2-3 of your top, reoccurring spiritual gifts, natural abilities and acquired skills. These are the ones you see most often in use. List in the box below.

SPIRITUAL GIFTS	NATURAL ABILITIES	ACQUIRED SKILLS
_____	_____	_____
_____	_____	_____
_____	_____	_____

FOUR PERSONALITY TYPES

Using the defintions on p. 27, with your partner answer the following questions by choosing which of the four-personality types is most like you. Make a check mark under one of the four responses.

SITUATION	TASK	INFLUENCE	TEAM	DETAIL
1. When I do a project I am...	___	___	___	___
2. When I am under pressure...	___	___	___	___
3. When I best contribute...	___	___	___	___
4. When others talk about me	___	___	___	___

© CRM/Terry Walling

Implementation
Linking Your Personal Calling to Your Calendar

Exercise

Calling >> Roles >> Yearly Objectives >> Monthly Goals

Step 1—Defining Yourself
Our goal should be to bring all of who we are to everything we do.
Ephesians 2:10 affirms that we each are God's workmanship, created in Christ Jesus to do good works.

Influence elements and personality type both help to express your uniqueness as God's created being. God gives to believers a variety of unique, life experiences to help clarify their identity and roles in the lives of others and the Body of Christ.

Influence Summary
Summarize your capacity to influence others and your personality in 1-2 sentences.

(Example: I am an influence oriented person who seeks to bring about change through leadership and exhortation gifts, and my abilities to catalyze change and build teams.)

_____
_____
_____

Step 2—Defining Your Roles
Life roles refer to those roles that are a part of who we are as people and often deal with the significant relationships in our lives. Place a ✔ by those roles that you are currently fulfilling. List others not mentioned. (Note the number and the potential of diffused focus.)

___ Father	___ Disciple	___ Homemaker	___ Business leader
___ Mother	___ Mentoree	___ Son	___ Teacher
___ Husband	___ Discipler	___ Daughter	___ Local church leader
___ Wife	___ Mentor	___ Sibling	___ Team leader
___ Student	___ Worshiper	___ Friend	___ Small Group Leader
___ Citizen	___ Civic leader	___ Helper	___ Sunday School Teacher
___ Counselor	___ Innovator	___ Team player	___ Intercessor
___ Servant	___ Catalyst	___ Networker	___ Pastor

Others: _____
_____

© CRM/Terry Walling

Exercise

What if you could only focus on SIX roles?
Which of the life roles best assist you in living out your calling?
Go back and review your Personal Calling Statement.

Select Life Roles that match your life situation and your statement of personal calling. Choose SIX Life Roles and give a one-line description of that role. (Make sure there is a balance of being and doing)

1. _____ _____
2. _____ _____
3. _____ _____
4. _____ _____
5. _____ _____
6. _____ _____

Step 3—Determining Your Yearly Objectives

Focused believer's establish yearly, end-result, benchmarks for each of their life roles. What progress do you want to make in the year ahead toward the accomplishment of your personal calling in each of your life roles?

Using your Personal Calling Statement (an in particular your statement of vision), write one-year, end-result statements that you hope to accomplish for each role.

Example:
Life Role—End-result
Leader—A new training system for our emerging leaders.
Husband—Identification and clarity of my wife's ministry and role.
Intercessor—Focused times of prayer for my family, our church and our community.

1. _____ _____
2. _____ _____
3. _____ _____
4. _____ _____
5. _____ _____
6. _____ _____

© CRM/Terry Walling

Monthly Goals

Example

Personal Calling Statement

I live to glorify my Lord and Savior, Jesus Christ through personal worship and inner-life growth, a lifestyle that adorns grace and truth, and by participating in the loving, winning and training of new believers who will lead the advancement of the church.

As a result of my calling and my own unique giftedness, I have committed my life to raising a family that loves God and models a genuine, believable faith. I desire to intentionally help my wife discover her place in ministry and grow in her effectiveness, spending the time building up, encouraging and empowering our children.

I also dedicate myself to extending the kingdom of God through refocusing mission-based, Christ-centered local churches, and developing relational support systems that will mentor and empower a new generation of leaders. I desire to impact 1000 churches and 1000 leaders into the 21st century.

Roles	Monthly Goals
Husband	1. Weekly time with Robin
	2. Find Gifts Seminar-material
Dad	3. Time with each child (2–3 hrs.)
Worshipper	4. Half-day prayer retreat
Leader	5. Training Booked--Call team
Pioneer	6. Develop new evangelism resource
	7. Meet with unchurched couples
Mentor	8. Contact Allan
	9. Explore mentoring with Peter

February

S	M	T	W	T	F	S
					1	2
3	4 10:30 Robin 1	5 9:00 Gifts-2 9:30 Train-5	6	7 8:00 Allen-8	8 2:00 Res. 6	9
10	11 10:30 Robin 1	12	13	14 3:30 Kyle-3	15	16
17	18 10:30 Robin 1	19 8:00 Peter-9 7:00 Meet-7	20	21 3:30 Sue - 3	22 9:00 Retreat - 3	23
24	25 10:30 Robin 1	26	27	28 3:30 Ruth- 3		

© CRM/Terry Walling

Step 4—Deciding to Integrate into Your Calendar

Take the challenge to move beyond great intentions!
Accept the challenge of organizing your next month's schedule according to your personal calling statement.

Example

From the example on p. 32, notice how a believer's yearly objectives were translated into monthly goals and integrated into his calendar. This is a proactive approach to scheduling. Other appointments will fill his calendar, but this helps ensure that each month he is intentional in accomplishing a facet of his personal calling, even in the midst of a busy schedule.

You may not be involved in church leadership, but you face the same challenge of living with a busy schedule. What would the next month look like if you were to approach these 30-days intentionally, based upon your calling statement?

Test It Out!

Before setting this aside, take the challenge.
After a four-week trial period, review the results. Decide how effective this system is for you. What can you adapt to make the process more effective?

Break down your yearly objectives on p. 31, into bite-sized monthly goals. Use the Planner (p. 34) to schedule an activity related to each of your roles. Feel free to make additional copies of the Planner as needed.

How to Keep Going

Set aside a one-hour regular weekly appointment with yourself. Review your activities from the previous week and revise your monthly calendar to accomplish your goals.

Monthly

Set aside a half-day block of time for monthly reflection, prayer, and planning to help maintain perspective and intentionalize your next month. Be sure to incorporate time for worship, prayer, and character growth into this half-day event.

Yearly

Once a year a leader should set aside a day to review the past year. Review what you've accomplished in each of your life and ministry roles, update and revise your five-year plan, and enhance your personal mission statement.

© CRM/Terry Walling

Monthly Goals

Planner

Personal Calling Statement

Roles	Monthly Goals

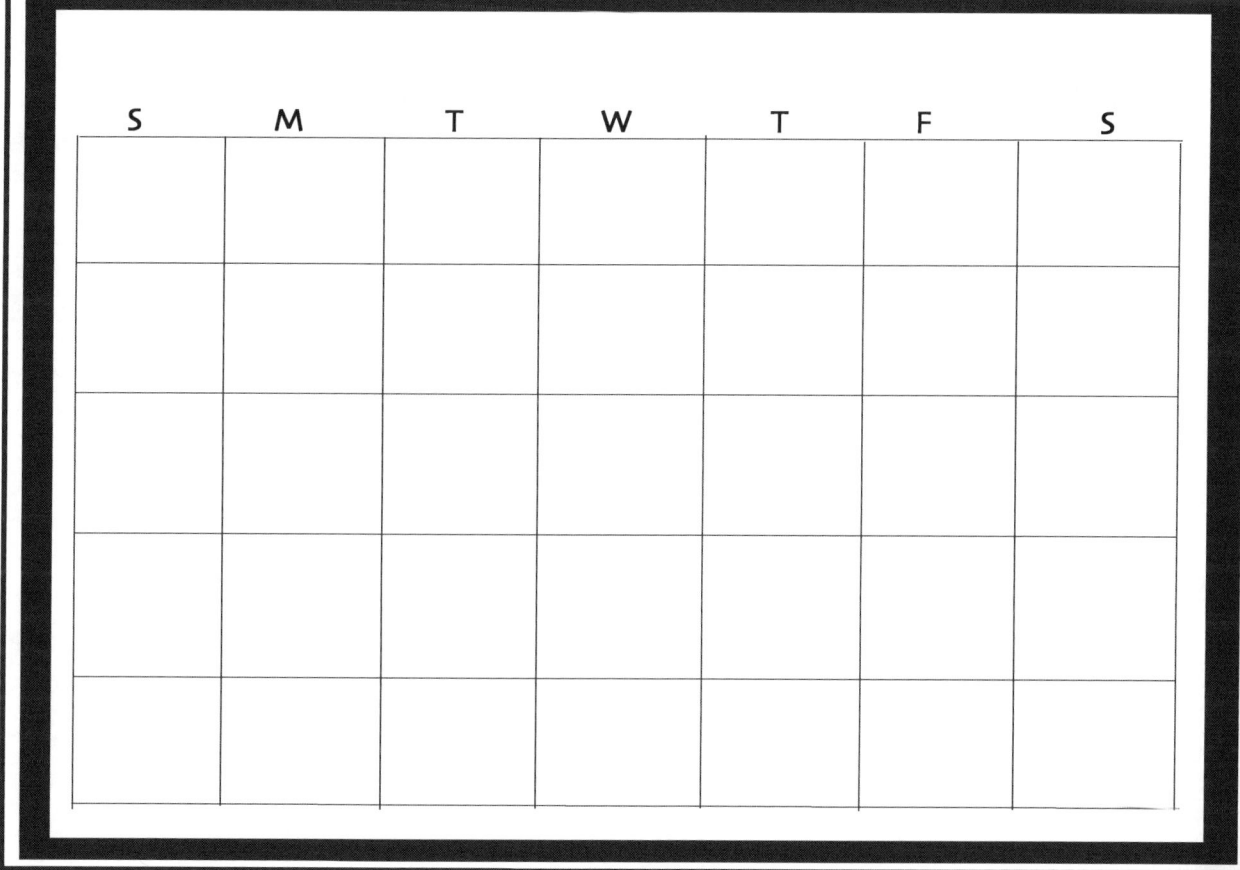

S	M	T	W	T	F	S

© CRM/Terry Walling

Focus
Next
STEPS

Where do we go from here?

A **personal calling statement** is an individual's best understanding to date of his or her future direction. Too often, believers attempt to chart a future course of action based upon their current state of affairs, without considering their past and without acknowledgment of their values.

Now that you have completed your calling statement, the next key to living a more focused life is to obtain mentors who can help ensure your ongoing development and accomplishment of your personal mission.

There is often more **personal mentors** available to you than you might believe. The key to locating mentors is understanding your actual mentoring issue(s) in which you need help, and identifying the type of mentor needed to help you address this issue.

The diagram found on p. 36 illustrates how this workbook, *Focus*, leads to **Mentoring**, and the next step in the personal development process called *Focused Living*.

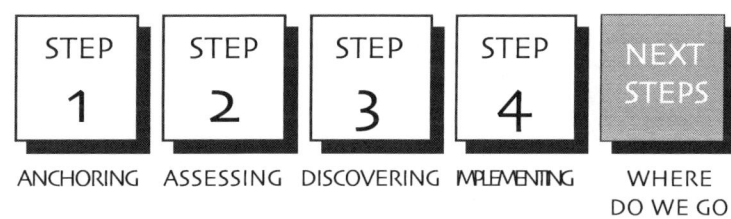

STEP 1 ANCHORING
STEP 2 ASSESSING
STEP 3 DISCOVERING
STEP 4 IMPLEMENTING
NEXT STEPS WHERE DO WE GO FROM HERE?

© CRM/Terry Walling

100-DAY PLAN

FREE RESOURCE AT LBU Store

www.leaderbreakthru.com/lbu

MOVE YOUR INTENT INTO NEW BEHAVIOR!

The 100-Day Plan

APEX focused on helping you clarify your contribution.

What happens next will help to determine if the time you invested in the APEX process will make any difference. What you do during your first 100 days by way of coaching and accountability will help to ensure long-term implementation.

The first 100 days after any breakthrough experience is key to securing the change and translating that experience into new long-term behavior for any leader.

Holistic Change… applying your results to each of the FOUR spheres of Influence:

Family: Arena of influence that includes parents, spouse, children, extended family, and friends.
Vocation: Arena of influence including your place of work, profession, career, and/or job opportunities.
Community: Arena of influence including your local neighborhood, city, county, or society at large.
Church Arena of influence that starts with your local church body and moves to the wider world.

The 100-Day Plan is an intentional implementation tool designed to help you secure the change that has occurred as a result of the APEX breakthrough experience.

The 100-Day Plan is a challenge to intentionally script the next 100 Days so you create short-term wins that reflect the gain you achieved from your Breakthru experience.

THE BEST PART IS THAT THE 100-DAY PLAN is a FREE RESOURCE.
DOWNLOAD THE FREE COACHING RESOURCES AND AUDIO PODCAST
at the Leader Breakthru website.

GO TO THE LEADER BREAKTHRU UNIVERSITY HOME PAGE AND CLICK THE RESOURCES BUTTON
OR, go to http://www.leaderbreakthru.com/resources/free-resources.php

THERE IS NO BETTER TIME THAN NOW TO GET STARTED!

www.leaderbreakthru.com

© Leader Breakthru 2015

Focused LIVING

Clarifying Calling

What is Focused Living?

Focused Living is a personal development discovery process that helps leaders clarify their life direction and personal calling.

Each of us is being shaped by God to make a unique and ultimate contribution (Ephesians 2:10).

The question is not whether God is at work, but knowing how to better recognize (1) what God is at work doing, and (2) how to set a course-direction to align with His work.

Over 20,000 leaders have experienced the Focused Living process in more than ten languages. It seeks to address three core questions:

Where have you been?

Where are you going?

Who can help you get there?

What are the take-aways?
1. Personal Timeline
2. Statement of Personal Calling
3. 100-Day Plan and link to Mentoring

Topic: Calling and issues of Identity and Direction

Who: For leaders seeking greater focus and clarity; can apply to leaders as early as 20s-30s.

What: Focused Living Retreat, Focused Living Small Group, and Focused Living On-LINE

Time: FL Retreat (8-Sessions of 1.5 hours)
FL SMALL Group (10 Sessions)
FL On-LINE (12–15 hours)

Resources: Focused Living Workbook

Focused Living On-LINE process

Focused Living Small Group Resource

Online: www.leaderbreakthru.com/training/focused-living-online/

Exercises: **Personal Timeline,** First Order of Calling (being), Core Values, Second Order of Calling (doing), Surrender, The 100-Day Plan

More Info: www.leaderbreakthru.com

LEADER DEVELOPMENT PATHWAY

Every Leader Needs...
SOVEREIGN *Perspective*

Transitions
Awakening (CALLING)
Deciding (CONTRIBUTION)
Finishing (CONVERGENCE)

**Focused Living
CALLING**
Clarity of
Direction

**APEX
CONTRIBUTION**
Discovery of
Unique ROLE

**Resonance
CONVERGENCE**
Choosing to
Finish Well

SITUATIONAL *Coaching*

Bite-Sized ONLINE video modules and worksheets delivered just-in-time to meet the immediate needs that all leaders face.

Through **Leader Breakthru University** leaders get the help, when they need the help, in the trenches as they face the challenges.

www.leaderbreakthru.com   LEADER | Breakthru

Made in the USA
Lexington, KY
17 October 2016